D0871872

MILK

Dorothea Lasky

MILK

Wave Books

Seattle &

New York

Published by Wave Books

www.wavepoetry.com

Copyright © 2018 by Dorothea Lasky

Wave Books titles are distributed to the trade by

Consortium Book Sales and Distribution

Phone: 800-283-3572 / SAN 631-760X

Library of Congress Cataloging-in-Publication Data

Names: Lasky, Dorothea, 1978– author.

Title: Milk / Dorothea Lasky.

Description: Seattle : Wave Books, [2018]

Identifiers: LCCN 2017036460| ISBN 9781940696638

(limited edition hardcover) | ISBN 9781940696645 (softcover)

Classification: LCC PS3612.A858 A6 2018 | DDC 811/.6—dc23

LC record available at https://lccn.loc.gov/2017036460

Designed and composed by Quemadura

Printed in the United States of America

9 8 7 6 5 4 3 2 1

First Edition

Wave Books 069

You should know
Because they were the sons of Mars
Without fear
They drank the milk not meant for them

OVID, *Fasti*

A FIERCE AND VIOLENT OPENING

Blood is gushing everywhere
From the lips of the bear's face
Out the elevators
The children's eyes
When they are taken down by the ax
The whole hotel is overtaken with blood

You know I've started to think
You really shouldn't say
Things you don't mean
The way you gushed into me
And then that woman
Who seems so much older, and isn't

Dear woman, I read your essay
That fate could have been me
Blood is gushing from between my legs
I can't feel a thing
No really
I can't feel a thing

When they propped me up
They said, oh, she's so strong
But I am not
I cry too
I cried for you
You left me, always, in the rain

Dear love, you were so brave
The blood exploded within you
You were that whole hotel
Could have been us
I gushed
Out came the blue-green cream

DO YOU WANT TO DIP THE RAT

Do you want to dip the rat
Completely in oil

Do you want to dip the rat
Before we eat it eat it

Do you want to dip the rat
Completely in oil

Before we eat it

Tender tender meat
Like pork shoulder

One hundred traps set
Eighty hanging in a row to be broiled

With you
I'd take it raw

Tiny pink feet
Glistening with oil

Legs and feet
Glistening with oil

Matted fur and face
Weighted down with oil

Everything in oil
But the teeth are shiny clean

No what I really want to know
Before you open that mouth again

Should we completely dip the rat in oil
Before we eat it eat it

Should we completely
Dip the rat in oil

Before we eat it

GHOST FLIGHT TO THE MOON

You were never what I thought
Don Repo, you fixed the ovens
Where they put the people
And stirred their bones to ash
Flight to the mountains
Then the descent
Landing gear
Billowing silver
Like fabric acorns
We left at the corner of the sky
What or what I say to you
I wish I saw you more
Is what I said
To no response
But you probably
Were thinking of something
Like about your taxes
Or the way you could cheat
Others out of the pool money
My friend once came over
And read me her poems so freely

I wanted to
But I couldn't abandon her
The silent unabated
No oxygen delivery
The feeling of no air
In the room
Thick with white steam
She sat at the corner waiting for me
Adorned in pink crystals
A sound stage
She said
You never write
I say no response
I say to give no response
Is to respond
My friend says
He says nothing
To say something
Building heavy with meaning
She says,
You are on fire
I look around
I say,
I know

A HOSPITAL ROOM

Morning walking is like a hospital room

The getting up and feeling sorry for sleep

Putting my fat body into a cab and going to the hospital

The smell of soup and pus everywhere

And not telling hardly anyone for fear they'd kill my child
like I almost had

Listening to my headphones, dreaming of surprise

Little ego in the hospital, does it care where you've been

We carry status, but it doesn't care

Still it pays for you to have an expensive room

And the nurses and everyone, they treat you better

A little extra cot, in the jail cell where they let you stay

And maybe the doctor is more invested to save you

If you flash some cash out your dressing gown

And it's winter, so you wash the stitches in Vaseline

Bathe the raw skin in marijuana, or some such thing

Eat turmeric because inflammation is

And the cells, they keep spilling

Or really, nothing more blank than your lifeforce

Or the promise of it

So you pray to that

Pray for that

Do you hear me

In the morning touching the wrist you will know what life is

His cold bald head in the winter air

How I wanted to rub it on my hands and kiss it

Instead I had to let him fly from tree to tree

Nothing more true than this

Eagle wrapped around this disaster for so many years

Nothing more unnerving than being a thing

Explorer in his fancy mud

Oh Behold, Behold

THE START OF THE FREE AND NATURAL

Dear friend you have a problem and it's called yourself

Dear self you have a problem and it's called yourself

Dear swamp demon you stole from me

Dear sky you have a night

The stars they go

Dear sun you have a problem and it's the light

Dear night you have a problem

I can't see anyone except the red music box

Dear love you see too much

I went to the wooden lake

I saw the wooden people

I took one out

It was a boy

It was wood and did not breathe

It had its wood hair grain

In a static wave

I breathed life into it

Its eyelids finally swung open

I told it it was once a tree

I laid it down I picked it up

Out its eyes came the clear liquid

But not tears, just humor
Just plastic utterances
Out its mouth came the words
But it wasn't alive yet
The stars in its absence, X-ed out
The middle sun, it shone
But only for me
Out your sink the bitter flowers
Oh, they have bloomed in the sewer
And the sewer flowers are jealous
Of what of what
How dare you ask
Obviously
The air

SAVE YOUR FLOWERS

Save your congratulations and your flowers
My baby is sunbathing on the moon
And with the eternal blue light she glows
In her clear house, with shutters
Save your kind regards, and visits
With doughnuts and kisses
Save your little nothings that amount to nothing
Save it save it
Purple green and christened blue
The flowers dug deep from hell
That you ring round my room
Another woman would have liked them anyway
Save your flowers and your missives
My skin is old and supple
But I am fair maiden only to my tiny vixen
Milking and milking, blue note on blue
Save your sadness and your leads of love
Your love won't hold me
Like a goddess uncuckcooned
Ill repute, little babe of udders
Stirring the inevitable

Dancing dancing
But not by myself anymore
Wrapping and wrapping the skin on the moon
So save your chrysanthemums and lilacs
Roses and tulips
Save your winter buds, and sun yellow weeds
I won't need them where I'm going
Brave icelet unbecoming
Praying only backwards
Praying praying on the moon

FLORAL PATTERN

I feel super needy today
The worst part of admitting this
Is that no one will care
This is the pattern I see
When I close my eyes too quickly
Not a pattern of being
But a floral pattern from the '70s
Yellows and oranges
You know social media
Is bad for me
People are too
I am thirty-seven and still a child
In my thinking about people
So I avoid them entirely
I smile
But that's about it
I'll never know anyone
Ego dissolving
Not anything
I will never be anything
But that's ok too

What if anything
On the beach the flowers are
What wild
What was ever wild
He wrote the last thing I could be
Not a relationship
But in art
He said what we were was art
Not a need
Not even an art need
What is an art need
So full of culture
What is a cultus
Coitus
My silly sublime
Bright turquoise palm flowers
Over a magenta hue
Palindrome in the night
Asking me
For my prediction
And upon divination
I said it was a great love in a museum
No I meant me
No I mean myself

Darling all night
I have been flickering off on off
Heavy as a lecher's kiss
The neon lights of the overlay
The room that will always be timeless
Not an intrapersonal concern
But an art one
The moon
No door
But a face in its own right
My mind
A bloodhound
For oblivion
Already in the house
Answer your phone
Call me
Call me I will answer
From inside your house
Dripping my wares everywhere
Answer me
Was I really so unreposed
Naked corpse
So slowly working
Answer me

Was I really so
Palindrome of shadow and light
Not a thing of worth
But a barmaid
That's all you wanted
In the lilac light
Where I gave up
My most sacred to you
Without a second's thought
And you answered the phone
From another sphere
Laughing
Laughing at me
Laughing

WHY I HATE THE INTERNET

When one is on the Internet
In the middle of fear
You can find a Mashable article
About abandoned shopping malls

Each image more horrible than the last
Each click to a burned-out neon room
To an article then
About Courteney Cox and Pennzoil

Why am I tired of the Internet
I have no friends here
I write down words in my room
For a thousand hours and no likes

So, instead of the Internet I will make a little shop
In an art gallery and tell no one
In my dirty leopard coat it will be 1992 forever
Burned-out hamburger sign in the foreseeable distance

Why am I tired of the Internet
Well where is my pussy, my old old pussy
No, my pussy belongs in the hallowed books of yore
Not in this time, or online

THE MISCARRIAGE

The doctor says it's an empty room in there

And it is

A pale sack with no visitors
I have made it and surrounded it with my skin
To invite the baby in

But he did not enter
And dissolved himself into the sea so many moons ago

I wait to see
Will the giant bean be in there another day

The women of the world say
Work harder!

The men in the world say
Work harder!

I work and work but I am an empty sack
Until I bleed the food all over the floor

Then I am once again with everything
Until the gods say, you've done well, good sir
You may die now

And the people who were asking me for favors all along
Knock on the coffin door
But I am gone, gone

THE BOOK OF STARS
AND THE UNIVERSE

I wish I could have explained to you what that looked like

The purple glow and time

This doesn't feel right anymore I said to him

Men thinking I'm very strange or silly

Women fighting me in the aisles

Louise said it was a mayhem she wanted

Louis you betrayed me, upon the moon

Max said the UFO is what brought him to the other side

In the dream my father took my dog

He brought her to the other world

My dog I miss you

My father I miss you

Max, I miss you

Oh poor me

My daughter you are mine to love

My house I love you once and for all

Time I love you

You're mine

You've always been

Time
You're mine
You've always been
Once and for all

THE CLOG

What stays in
Doesn't come out
Nipples hard with milk
When things are of another time
They are of that time
Not timeless
They are no longer here
Nipples hard with liquid or falsities
White and soft
I can't get it out
No matter how hard I yank
Or pull and suck
Face watching with my own
Nipple in my mouth
Like the room she's in
I went and I seduced
But no matter what
I couldn't get her to leave
Aqua and in the morning, coffee
The bathroom gold and green
No matter what I said

She stayed there
She had her own fantasies to wait for
Milk that never comes out
It grows inside
Does it fold back in time
I want to say it becomes different
The man who grafted another face
What poems I wrote for him
No I want to say
That when you came at me
With the syringe
That I loved you
In gold and green
You came at me
Revision upon revision
Of your love
It wasn't like you
To give up
I knocked and knocked
And you went back
Into your doorway
What days
The nipples rising
With future things to come

What happened to those thoughts
To those people
I loved that woman
In the building
Sunset road
The place
With the dead babies
But no matter what I did
How hard I yanked
She would never leave
I knocked and knocked
No matter what I did
Or said
I just couldn't
Get her out of there

THERE IS NO NAME YET

Until I find a name
I will not put it in the soul calculator
I will leave it free and open and unnamed
And not limit my expectations for the kind of person
That goes in one direction of the wind
I will keep all lines of the wind open
And place all my days free and empty
And reenvision what it means to be unencumbered
Or bereft
Not crying but the expanse of numbers
That go beyond the grave to what is left
And it may be true
I said it could be true
That the sunny days do stick to walls
And then enter you
It may be true that the purple bells do chime
Every day you let them
It may be true that the sweet juice
I put across my lips would not be my last
But that the nights could get better and better
Until the evil is banished until the day

When the sun would crush it anyway
It was true without a set of things like letters
It was true the air was free and open
And I saw things as they were
Without violence
For the first time

MILKING THE REST OF IT

Turn the faucet on
Turn the breast on
Emptied completely of milk
With the tiny hoses in a row
Emptied of when the ships were she
Child of my heart
A dull ache and then
No pain at all
When the muzzle found my mouth
To not let the milk form a crust
Of ice and sugar
On the nipple
And to put the cap on it
Emptied of
The ships where she
Eight tiny roses in a row
Where water goes in
The greenish water
Where the saints
Can grow
You know some will tell you

No you're already happy
But the trap of your life
Is that you're trapped in this body
And even though you search
For twenty to eighty years for the demon
In other people
Turn the faucet on
And look in the mirror
The demon
Is you
Dull milk
Aching out the little faucets
In your nipple
To go nowhere
There's no baby
There's no mother
Just an endless hallway
Of fear upon fear
Neverending tinted roses
All in a row
The lavender water
We sip on a chilly day
Before we go
On our way

Six tiny horsemen
In moon suits
Leading us not to the promised land
But to a box
Where our reward for surviving this mess
Is to die and then forget
And inside the box
The greatest tormentor of them all
She's there
To hang you by the teeth
And say
There's no baby
There's no mother
Ice cold and stiff
Hacked
And hewed
Me and you
Except thank fully for me
Goodbye hello
Milky one
I'm gone
I'm home
I'm gone
Goodbye
Except thankfully for she

Goodbye milk
Hello love
Nice to meet you tiny faucet
Hello milk
No
Goodbye milk
Goodbye life
Hello life
Goodbye hello
Death
Death
All of it
Death and more death
Goodbye where they roast
The people in the urn
Where they shut the oven door
Before the baby can get out
Help help
I feel the curse
Burning my baby
The dull milk ache
Oh the pain the oak
No no
Goodbye pain
Goodbye

MILK, NO. 2

I keep doing this past what is pointless
I keep doing it past what is good
I rise, and I am not sick anymore
But you are sleeping, breath falling
It is 8 a.m. somewhere
Maybe in L.A.
Where my brother sleeps, fitfully
In arms of sundress
Maybe where my mother lived
Her whole life and got the sun in her too
I think back to what I was ten years ago
Maybe twenty, the people
Great Aunt Ida told me
To live this one
The dreams they say of men
I paint their eyelids as always
In what colors
Of course, the greens
I just keep making these things
Past the point of what is normal
I look for faces but the eyes are dead

But when you look at me, I can't lie
Baby, it's with love
I never knew what it was to be this way
But then again I never let myself be
Cascade of ocean
The beach was lost and dark
The house was dark dark
I went in, I wasn't scared
It wasn't the going in the door that struck me
It was the getting out, or even wandering
What's behind the hidden doors
Can I find a bed there
Can I set up my electronic things
Can I put this machine on
It's my armor to protect you
I have nothing
You are in a glass house
The fall of it
Orange hearts one after the other
My true love is sleeping
I tell him, don't rest
I swirl
I find another
Another with the moon

He writes me letters,
The sweet bees are for you
Twenty-nine bees
Like a beekeeper
No it is the bees who are my lovers
For them I am but a flower
I enter the scene
For the bees, I am magenta forever
I enter the scene, not the house
It's easy to be brave
The house is not glass, it's plastic
It's clear and hot
I can see you, Flower
I can see you simply
Your head
And it's bursting
With colors no one knows about
I can see you, Animal
You breathe
And it's not to raise the dead
I read, and it's to find the breathing
I read to my baby
About the things
Milk, it connects

Milk it is not cum
A kind of off-white blood
Not an aftereffect
I squirt all over the sheets
My lifeforce
Not blood, but cum
Milk is not what the air gives
It is what you are
You say you let yourself go
Maybe you didn't
Maybe you should squeeze out
Everything you have
My true love he is awakened
By the flooding of it all
Not blood but me
When I leave
I'll leave behind not this stain
But this jewelry of being
I'll put in a vial the frozen things
My baby, you died before it all began
Then you lived
And lived longer
I gave you all I had
Who wouldn't

This isn't a story you know
This isn't an article, I'm sure
I'm sure of it
This isn't the going in
This is what is out
I squeeze and all the lifeforce
I am not shell, or what I would have assumed
I am snake again, and I can make it a hundred times
True love you sleep on dark red sheets
I bleed everywhere you drink me
It is off-white and iron-filled
We read love letters
Written by the bees
They write of black and blue flowers
They are bursting
In ways we could not see
You kiss me and I squeeze out the orange flowers
In a clear house we and the pansies
Butterflies and bees
Blood red milk
It's drinkable
You drink me
And I am no longer me
But lifeforce

Blood and bones

Peach

Peaches, and the palm trees

The sun, the beach

Blood red bees

That when I speak

The burn

Hot ash yellow flower

In a clear house

Baby when you breathe

I can feel you sleeping

All alone, darkening rose

I rise, no longer me

No, once I thought it was over

I didn't go in

I went out

Arrows going away from the center

Not quarterly, but to see

Ash is not cum

Blood red cum, milking

Breathing milk, breathing bees

Blood red bee

He flew

Into the hothouse flower

It was clear

It was not to cum

Yellow pansy

It was to see

LOVE POEM FOR BATHSHEBA

In the very oddest picture
There is a split
On one side, a girl with a blank expression
On the other, a girl with a smile
That is maniacal
She is the same girl
There is a mirror
The smiling face
In the reflection
It's so odd
One girl, made into two

Why is a knowing smile so evil
I ask myself
And do not say
The question aloud
For fear that they will hear me

All this talk about haunted spaces
But it's the body
That's haunted

With double dreams
And double doors
The double-cream

It's the silly truth that's haunted
And when I couldn't speak I spoke
And when I couldn't wake I woke
And when I couldn't hear her anymore
That grating voice
She was gone

Bathsheba Sherman
Bathsheba Sherman
In the movie of you
They made you a jew

Always a jew
When you want a cunt of pure evil
When only an evil cunt will do
People, sure why not
Why not why not
Always make her a jew
With her lokshen kugel
With her taroc pack

With her taroc pack
With her ich ich ich

Bathsheba they hung you
Baby, they'll hang me, too
Me and you
Who is that?
Who is that?
It's us
Dumb face
Arms filled with blue

No who is that
It's not us
It's me and you
It's me and you

When only a really evil cunt will do
That's the mistake
The world makes
Pure evil, brute evil
Through and through

Oh who is that
Who is that
The one in the doorway
Face coming through

That's the mistake
The world makes
Dumb face
That's us

Oh who is that
Who is that
That's me and you
That's me and you

THE GHOST

I saw him
His body a very pale sea, almost green
Soaring above me in a different sphere
With gold wings
He had a blissful expression
One maybe he never had
Certainly he was always smiling, somewhere
When he died
I had just gotten betrayed by a friend
I thought was mine
I forgave him
Was more just said
You live through any of it
But what is the red shoulder we long to see
I thought that I too would reach a great canyon
My arms and legs blissed out
Instead I blossomed inside
Oh I loved his wife and children
But they were still here with me
When my father died he went straight up to heaven
When the ghost died he stayed with us for a while

I forgot to mention that the wings were gold and green
And the winds were heavy
They held his body
Afloat in air as if in the ocean
I forgot to say that when it was summer
I too measured the red bell heads
I said the hell with it
All of it
Heavy air will you hold me
Suspended in the ocean of time
Where I will never see you again
My skin gold and green
Sweet king, you left us
I know it
Dark is dark
The darkness, darnit
It surrounds
With heavy air
Arms and legs suspended
The head

THE GHOSTS

Anne Sexton's ghost just said, I'm watching you
Then sent me to her Book of Beasts
What is a Ghost
A light peppery air being
Or a solid, jelly thing
The book
I've died before
But no one believed me
And I came back here
To haunt my beloved
Then breathing
And we washed in words, now dead again
Now back again, I am no longer jelly
I'm water, a peachy lilac color
Both born into blue
For someone or something could be watching
Some are watching as I write this
The ghostly comediennes I share this speech
Or, you know that hum
That goes and flows
That's ghosts

Who will be reborn eventually
The trick is to make friends with all of them
The trick is let the darkness out into the moonscape
And funnel the light into one strong sound
Only I can hear the sounds of my ancestors
But you can too
What is a ghost
A ghost is a mountain
It's green it's frightful
It's written in Latin
But not the kind we read anymore
What is a ghost
It's a flower
Big and weeping with purple colors
A weeping world, not vacuous
What is a ghost
It is my father
It is my dog
It is a dream
I dream of people
Do they or do they not exist
If you think this world exists
Then I think you do too
If you think you are breathing now

Then I promise the ghosts breathe down upon your neck
What is a life
If it's longing, then fuck it
Sister, take me back to the beach
Let's watch the sunset and then the moon
If it's only this then put on my mask
And send me wheeling down the halls
I'll spend the rest of days
Talking only to the children
If children are ghosts
Then put the capes upon them
And paint their eyes with terracotta
Then make them cakes all day long
Then tie the brightly colored streamers
If babies are ghosts then have many of them
Then make the new new again
If you are a ghost then let me kiss you
And feel your faintest undertone
If spring is ghostly then take me in it
Then leave me in the fields until I'm eaten
By bees and breads
Until I can come here
Come here clean again
Wheel me down the halls

I'm old I'm old
Give mercy to my sisters, the bees
But not to me
I'm not old
I'm young
Always young
Oh youth
Won't you go already
Same drone
From here to neverending
Bathing spirits
Submerged in blue light
Acid lake
I'll sink in
In hot pink outlines
No
Behold
The wooden lake
I'll sink in
Again

THE WAY WE TREAT THEM

We make the elderly into prisoners
Giving them a white suit
To be transported from one place to another
Discriminating because of background
Discriminating because of cancer
Unbearably hard
Unbearably cruel
The moon

You think I haven't seen
But I too have carried that card
From the admissions department
After a whole life you survived
Neon rainbow streak of pink neon green
Bright yellow streaked in a diagonal
On the face of the acorn
The tiny seeds which are the enemy of light

The way we see them is a measure
Of what soul we have
I'll go so far as to say we have none

Now seeing what I've seen
And the ways in which
We shutter the orange acorn
And the ways in which
We take the very painted hand to the butcher

People don't live until the end to be healthy
But you can't even pay someone to hug you
You can't pay someone to love you
Even then when
Please what kind of weather
We shut the doors and give little plates
And ask them to beg for a doorway
To rest their hands

The super vision
We ask them to pay us
Before we let them leave
The butterflies and pansies are for Helen
The double-cheeked cat
All day long the brick wall
With its indefinable orange
My advice to you: stay strong, stay young

BECOME A PERSON

The bee died upon entering the water
What happened to his honey no one knew

I left one fig and one kumquat
In each dish for the host

There were the yellow trunks of trees
The memory of Spain

There was the memory of being
The memory of love

Let the water take you in
So your neck is just a stalk, the head blooms

Let everything go away
You are a person

Be a person
Become a person again

The happiest he ever made me
The table in white

Whereupon we list the white seashore
The White Sea, the white seahorses

They said I loved him better than anyone
The white seashore

No I never knew him
The bees

The bees
They know everything

Be a person
Be a person again

ME AND YOU

You know that scene
In an old Freddy movie
Where there is that junkie
She's kind of a punk
And seems tough
But with that mere surface-level punk vulnerability
She's wearing all silver and black
They are in an alley
She says, fuck you Freddy
And brandishes a knife
He looks at her, alarmed
Then lifts his arms
Wanna get high, he says
Each finger a syringe filled with bright blue
On her arms
Little pockets and mouths
Open
Beckoning
What does he do
He falls forward, with intent
And she knows

What she's in for
Who is that?
That's me and you
Who is that?
That's me and you

IF YOU CAN'T TRUST THE MONITORS

If you can't trust the monitors
Then why do they have the monitors
If you can't trust the cars
Then why have the cars
If you can't trust that I think you're hot
Then why do you look so good
Turning me on that way that you do
If you can't trust the people
Then why have the people
If you can't trust the cards then why have the cards
If you can't trust this room then why have the room
Why not just an open space
Where you can be naked and fascinating
If you can't trust the milk in the bottles
Then why have the bottles
If you can't trust the wine the song
Then why have the country
If you can't trust the kangaroo
Then why go jumping
If you can't trust the sky
Then why have the sky at all

What good the moon and stars
If you can't trust the stars
Then why look out
Why not just sit in your room
It's dark and safe anyway
If you can't trust what's dark and safe anyway
Then why even bother
Then why even be here at all
I don't know
I just went and walked
But desire is hopeless
If you can't trust the windowsill
Then why put the flowers there
Why not leave it bare
Oh I did
And then what
After a while
Anyway
That old sun
It burned it green
The windowsill
And when I returned to the room
All I saw was green
Grass green

Like grass but greener than
A halting hue of it
And I forgot the flowers
And I forgot you
If you can't trust the daybreak
Then why have the daybreak
Why not sit
Let the night come
It won't stop itself
The hormones
And all

HOT PINK SUMMER TITTY TASSELS

Everyone wants to negate the work of women
And yet we are all here
Cause some woman held us in her abdomen
For some ungodly amount of time
And then pushed us out
Or had them slice her pussy into bits
Or even cut her open and leave her to die
While a group of people sucked and smoothed
Our ever lying countenance
You say in your adolescent nightmares
Well then I wish you never had me
But isn't it too late for that
You're here
And you look at things
And forward that to the things you say
Still the books by women about women
Don't win awards
If anything put a cigarette in there
A martini
Pretend to be a man
I like vagina jewelry not only on my vagina

But things made out of resin
And wood
That look like the unearthly glow
He told me, I like those hot green booby fringes
I said you do but would you wear them
He said no but make me a ring
Of that hot pussy and I will wear it
All the day long
So I did
And he did
Nice vagina man
Wearing my pussy on his finger
You know sometimes
Sometimes
You win

TWIN PEAKS

I'm sadly just pure instinct in a jean jacket
A guess in a red dress
I only have time for coffee
But do you
Have time
For me

Shadow cousin
With the face
Of my past abuser
Cough cough and a little
Whatever

My pussy squirts flowers
In the spring
Purple hair
And all that jazz
Like a tear

The moon is in Scorpio
I'm

In
The moon
My
Baby
Moon
My baby

I am still
Despite it all
Milking
Do you want me
Do you want to
Sip my clear
Cocoon
Full of nutrients

Sadly still only a
Summative
Mountaintop
Do you want to soak it
Completely in oil
Before we eat it
Glistening
The tiny pink feet

Do you want to soak
The rat
Completely
In oil
Before
We eat it
Eat it

You know you're such a mess
In a red dress
For you
I'd take it raw
Tell me
Do you want to soak the rat
Completely in oil
Before we
Eat it

Do you want to
Soak the rat
Completely in oil
Before
We eat it

OCD

What is a life like to not have to constantly accumulate a residue
Blue cheese spread on toast, with jam
Oh but it's all so delightful
To squirt my juices on the bed
Find splatters on the windowsill
In my mind I do not see the things that make me sick
But the constant accrual of the divine
I loved him
And he never brushed his teeth
And when he smoked
They grew worse and worse
Jagged pieces of glass, like a meth head
Sharp and rotting, but not of cock
My own teeth, with their film
Had to be burnished and branded
In a warehouse with others
While she stood over in lilac with her yellowy hair
Your semen and neon orange popsicle sauce
All over the bed
Your spaghetti supper, ornate with excessities

Loosing the bedsheets
The sign on the door:
Butterflies and pansies are for Helen
The turning and turning of excellence
The forgotten world: I forgot

KILL MARRY FUCK

It's a game
Have you ever played
One for each
I'll start:
Jack Nicholson in The Shining
Jack Nicholson in One Flew
Jack Nicholson in his bathrobe
It's blue
Kill Marry Fuck
Amy Winehouse
James Merrill
Freddy Krueger
Goodbye
Kill Marry Fuck
Ellen DeGeneres
Ellen DeGeneres's personal assistant
Phil Collins
Ashton Kutcher
A rainbow
My rapist
And Big Bird

Yeah
I'd fuck them all
But only Ellen DeGeneres
And only in that sailor suit
Ok, one more
Kill Marry Fuck
The postman
An isosceles triangle
My eggs
I mean my ovaries
Sunday afternoon in the park
With eggs
Not my ovaries
Wait, hold on
Do you want me
I want
Fish
A shining magenta clownfish
The taste of milk, sweeter than a cow
Jacking you off
In the yellow chair
With too many dressers
Kill Marry Fuck
All of it

And none of it with you
None of it with you or Charlie Sheen
Bill Clinton
Your leg in the air
Flopping in time
The dream of the unrecited
Me in the bathroom
And everything
With serial killers
With daffodils
You going down on me
In the back of a cab
Me shampooing your head with pine
No you hate oral sex
My breasts
Oil on your head
20 seconds
40 seconds
60 seconds
Sixty years later
A bomb of women
An entire country of women
Two women in the countryside
A pale green tapestry

Washed white by the seashore
The world
Kill Marry Fuck
A white star
The red dwarf
Time
I'd fuck time
I'd marry red
I've married anything
Holy Holy
Matrimony
Fiestaware
I'd kill them all
I have
Holy Holy
Day
The day that she was born
The intensity of birth
The incessant witch
It's over
So over
It never began
Jack Nicholson
Jack Nicholson

Jack Nicholson
Kill Marry Fuck
All of it
All of it
Or Jack Nicholson
Jack Nicholson
Whatever there is to do
I'd do it to you
The yellow kitchen
A knife
A veil
Jack Nicholson
In your blue robe
I'd do it
All of it
For you

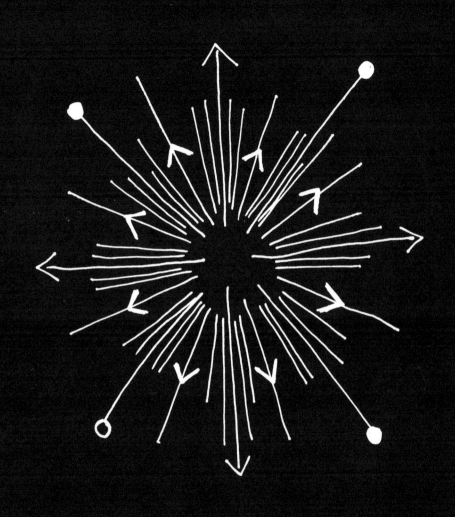

AT NIGHT THE SNAKES

At night the snakes go
Whack whack whack

At night the snakes go
Whack whack whack

She sits alone
In an easy chair

Easy to sit
Inside the snakes

At night the snakes
They go, whack!

It is easy to sit
All night and day

The snakes
Inside the letters

The snakes go
Whack whack whack

Inside the darkness
The snakes

They go
WHACK!

THE DREAM

A week after Max died I had a dream.

It was a late dream, after at least 5 a.m.

I woke up after.

In the dream, I was getting some sort of therapy and went to this woman's house.

She had this big garden and someone told me to wait there.

At first it looked just like plants and flowers and stone things.

Then all of a sudden I realized there were monsters everywhere.

Large snakes and lions.

Mutated animals, with rough reptilian parts where there should have been soft ones.

I got very scared.

I said, I don't think I want this kind of therapy.

The woman came into the garden.

She scooped me up like a baby and held me.

I closed my eyes.

A large animal came up to me and bit me on the left arm, but
did not sink his teeth in.

He just held my arm and I said to her, can't you make him stop.

Weren't the animals ostensibly hers.

She said, he thinks you are his dinner. He has forgotten he has
eaten.

Then she told me to slowly slide my arm from his mouth.

I could feel his teeth then go towards my side and I thought,
oh no, the baby.

Yesterday when the ultrasound machine found the tumor.

I thought of those summer days going to see her on my own.

Obsessions about him, who never did call.

Taking the subway to see her and then she was there.

When we saw into the machine now it was just a lush animal.

It didn't care. It had its own principle.

I woke up from the dream with the therapist still holding me.

But knowing that poems are things we can put on shelves.

I wanted to tell them: it's a miracle any of us are living.

But the moon and red stars had grown blasphemous.

The miracle had become the enemy once again.

The real life.

It's wild.

The monsters will bite you.

But only in dreams.

When you wake up she is holding you.

Corpse in the bath, with her disintegrating arms.

As lonely as the milk river.

That extends from here.

Deep feeding.

And far.

LITTLE KINGDOM

Everybody has a little kingdom
Where they can tell you what to do
So says the Enfamil lady
Who legally cannot say
What is best to feed the baby
So says you in your little house
A bit of pear juice
A cinnamon flower
So says the night that houses the day
Everyone has a little dominion
With which they can tell you you're wrong
When they enter your space
They can say what you have done with it
Just isn't what they would have done
They can use the towels you were
Saving for after the bath
For their feet
Their dirty dirty feet
And after they go
You'll have to spread their foot juice
All over your stomach and nipples

And say to the baby
Eat eat
We are no better than those
Who walk the earth
And the worms we ingest will make us strong
Everybody has a patch of dirty
Where they plant their green peril
Everybody makes the sign of the star
On their forehead
To let the devil know
It's me, Lord, it's me
Come home

THE SCHOOL

I am learning to be stubborn again, Max
A letter to Eileen
Written in the middle of winter
Or an ice block
Where I found myself
Haunted once again
Dear Eileen
I remember in a summer
Visiting you, with the dogs
And later there was ice cream
And one of the dogs bit me
But before all that I said, I want to start a school
And you smiled, good
Dear Elizabeth, you sit in a room
You are teaching me to be gold
Unbeknownst to the number 41
Where it was summer by a lake
And I said, this is it
Where in the middle of the ocean, I drowned
But then by some miracle
The one green crowning left itself for me

And the moon was bright and I could see my way backwards
To when I had jumped from the boat into the blackness
The School was supposed to be for poetry, not greed
I said to anyone, but no one cared
It's not that people don't care about greed
It's that, is that so surprising
And well, don't you have your own
Eileen, when you end a sentence with which
What should be a question mark but is a period
Well what could be better than that
A long plane ride
And then I found myself in the rain too
And I couldn't stop it, it just kept gushing
When one thing is wet can it get more wet
I mean when you are sopping with liquid
Can you get even more
The skin keeps so much of it inside
It keeps it outside too
I knew blue
But it didn't know me
And I am afraid of that
Dear friends that summer I grew a pair
Of anything
And I did not let myself enter a force

But I took the odious seaform
Into my bed
I said, lie down, oh vacuous one
Then I made love to that undulation
Then with what everyone said was frozen
I said was just very clean
And then with what everyone said had been lost
I said what is losing
I pressed the tiny dead flies to the pages of the book
And we bought a building
And I pretended it was the past
And Robbie you opened up the doors
And in the room was green light
And you said, oh stop it, you can be happy now

SNAKES

Serpents are a holy green

Halos on the bottom of the earth

Very slittering creatures

But there is a spirit to things

What is a snake and why is it important?

Imperial feminism

The medical profession

You should be speaking at my funeral, kid

Healing is not shameful

There is no shame in healing

There is no shame in getting better

All those healthy children

The time in-between

When you feel that poetry is the last thing you need

That's the time you need poetry most of all

Time is fierce

Pussyfoot doggerel

Fierce winds of it

In this life

There is always time

To make a comeback

Said I, the poets, with their branding

Oh write what you are, poets

Everyone's a snake

Most of all, including you

You have to steel yourself

From the garden

Be who you are poets

Cold creatures

With no other thought

But to thrive, then kill

THE MINOTAUR

The moon in the house is Room 237
Room No. 42
On 2/21 when my dreams became real
The moon smashed into the light
I spread my life like cards in front of me

If I die and all I have are these fucking poems
At least I will have the Moon Room
And the smooth black bedspread
Where I can sleep with a corpse
Who laughs at me, but still loves me after all

In this life I have had to go straight into hell
And no one gave me spring
Except you, but you were not real
Just like my family
Just like the moon

No the big bull has led me into this house
And I will have to kill him in order to get out of here

And after I do
What will I have but the morning that brings me no relief
And the day which brings no love at all

No really I would
Rather sleep in a bed with a corpse
And meet the horrendous spirits in the house
Than be here alone
In the middle hour

Waiting to find my destiny
Just waiting to go to the moon
When I have already traveled past it
Into the vast landscape
Where the dead are already dying

The yellow-striped cave
Kelly green and white rocks with fabricated craters
Where the mint bathroom
Is not to wash the soul clean, but to wash these trappings
Over and over again

FUCK EVERYONE

I want to sleep
But before I do
I'll ask the regular questions:
Why do women post their ultrasound photos
On Instagram
I don't expect an answer
I would never put the image so sacred for all
The enemies to see
Psychedelic rugs
In the movie
Before we cross over the bedroom
And into the little three stairs
Where she waits in a tub
To forsake us all
Beautiful greening body
And the way it hangs off the skeleton
Like an apron making way
Off the hips of the woman
Holding a tiny seed in her abdomen
If I water that flower
Should I fill my skin with jelly

Go to the hospital and beg for the sonographer
To take a photo of the fetus
Should I put it up for strangers
Later when I have a video of my baby
Looking so adorable, should I put it up
Look I flushed my eggs with venom
And cooked this human omelet
Am I a witch of feathers
I motherheathen must ask the public
I motherlover with my maternalpornography
Later when my little child
Is wearing her sailored dress
Should I say, look I'm just like you
I'm rich, I'm happy, I made this thing, I'm right
No mental illness, no disease, no poverty, so white
No unhappiness—this little person loves me
I'm everything, I'm night
Or should I keep her picture in an album
So that it can wash away with everything
In the water, in the solemn water
No fuck you all
You never gave a fuck about us
Goodnight

THE SECRET LIFE OF MARY CROW

Oh why the odor of decay sets the body / trembling.
We pretend we don't like / sensitivity of the anus, smell
of armpits. / After cooking, taking out the garbage—
. . . Penis moving, among guts, / membranes, juices.
Gills of the vagina / opening, closing. —MARY CROW

I am happy to say my dreams of the ancient worlds have
   returned
When I went there with my cat mask on
Music for the sake of music
Snow that was not real
Water that is not
The bees
The secret life
And secret promises
We make to the dead
Before we move our way over
I moved the lantern, the desk
The freight train
Magic for the sake of it
I made the water black and gold

For you to swim in it, my love
But you were still a child
Not real
But released
Into another's arms
Almost for
An eternity
The secret life of Mary Crow
Is one where we are no longer us
But the beginning of things
Forever

O

I didn't go to the land of glittering lights
And cold mornings
To protect you
My baby Mary Crow
Who sits in my stomach
Fluttering its heartbeat
Like a wild boar
In the jungle of a bridge
The lights flashing
Before all the teenagers succumb to wounds

Inflicted by the family
Mary Crow, you've seen it all
And all the nostalgia of my youth
My life
Did not prepare me
For the next level over

●

The night came and went
Before I was supposed to go
We all have leaves
We are all under that milk sleep
At six o'clock in the morning
We all take a risk for love
Mary Crow, I'd never risk you
For the empty shtetl of my great-grandmother
I'd never risk your heartbeat for the lonely flight of another
    halfway hello to everyone
I am looking for the real thing
Now I watch and watch under the red bridge
And I find the princess who was once you and isn't anymore
I understandably
Take my steed to the corner road

And knock upon the house of my bride
And say, Mary Crow
I am here
Won't you let me in

Maybe it's all fabricated
Maybe it's all a farce
The woman in the window is not Mary
We name her Susan or Sybillance
We name her Anne
We got her a good stocking
Before we shoved the light out
I can't write anymore
I don't speak
The once twice beloved he writes me mantras to himself
But not full of blood
They are the flat sentences of his youth
They are the empty periods
That cut everything in two
They are everything I have always given up
To be another person
They are green daddy and rich mayabell

They are the poem after the person
I can still hear him reading in the dark
After they turned the lights out

When a person dies
They usually find the body on the floor
It's true
All things fall as low as they can go
I know I too have gone
Thud in the last bit
Not from carnal knowledge
But from my love of you
Which is vast and unknowing
Beyond book and crypt keeper
Which is beyond light
I know the striped clock
The ghost clowns keep before the dull chill
Right before they take your teeth out
And rock your corpse upside down
To see the teeth fall
I know the body is a corpse and text
But is also a possibility

I know all the things they said
I really listened, despite it all

In the early days my friend
Thinking of the embryo
Put a baby elephant in a sack
And sent a picture of it to me
The moon dream
Then a cheetah and a lion
He put a tiny baby in a balloon
I took my skin and packed it around me
And ate a tonic full of vegetables for health
To fill my veins with vitamins
You have to stay you say
And you stop up my blood with an unhealthy cork
And this you say, this is natural
Before you put to bed our dreams and hopes
And what they were for anyway

I know in that moment
When I reached the uneven hour
I thought of my own blood pulsing
And yours papery
Like a lance
Like something that doesn't go anywhere
Like my friend's big dick
Like the children's playing cards
I thought of tarot
Which is a kind of blood
And I don't have friends anymore
I just wait and watch
For the underscorer to make his match in the sun
The girls unapologetic for what they've become
My own sorry for not doing the job like I said I would
But what if I had known
The dreams that would befall
If I had only known
You Mary Crow
Would come into my life so suddenly
Oh Mary Crow
Mary Crow

In the uneven night
When I should have been on
The freight train, with my many colored packages
They said he got locked into stomach care
So I stayed in my empty room
I don't want to shit or dream
Til I have this thing inside of me
Which might be the woman
We all hold
Maybe I'll go
Maybe that's what's left of me
Maybe I will be quiet in the yellow
And no one will talk to me
Maybe I will finally go on a date
After all
With the wild German man
Who holds a golden cross
As a plan for all beginnings
Maybe there is not a beginning
Even I can hold

Music for the sake of music is what they say to you

When the cutting has begun

You are not you anymore

In this form

And if you made a baby that has transformed

From two things

You can make a thing that is many things at once

We struggle

To know this

It's just what is

Still such a loser you are

Still how the season has changed

And will never be again

And vulnerability is imminent

Like the stroke

Like when the brain blooms

Like when the sterile room

Like when they put the tulips in my room

I said, who are they from

And they were from myself in another life

So red and horrible

Against the white landscape

Of my sorrow

Mary Crow I told you I didn't want anything
But you came back instead
To make me a piece of you
Magic for the sake of magic
And the end
Which is slightly off-putting
And the end which is like the night
But the dark and light is not the night
And the night which is not the end
And the beach in which we walked
So many lifetimes ago
I was another person
Actually
When I opened the door and said
This is new
And it was
And it's new
It's new again

YOU THOUGHT

You thought I'd flipped the switch and I hadn't
You thought I'd left the window open
And I wouldn't
You thought I'd turn the dial up
But I didn't
You thought I'd ring the sun the super
But I shouldn't
You thought I'd unlock the beehive
But I wouldn't
You thought I'd sing the dirge
But I couldn't
You thought I'd cook the rabbit
And I hadn't
You thought I'd come back that day
And I didn't
You thought I'd tend the flowers
But I couldn't
You thought I'd turn the lock
But I hadn't
You thought I'd open the door
See you

But I couldn't
You thought I'd lay down
But I couldn't
It kills me still
I couldn't
I couldn't

WINTER PLUMS

She's gonna die

We all are

Until then, the weather

The cold sweet fruit

That I kept for months

In the freezer

The vision

But not the skill

Is what I've mastered these days

Walking in the leaves by myself

To listen to the trees and what they say

Is more interesting

And more important

Than talking

Shut up

Live

People argue for the sake of daylight each day

Even they

Know more than the trees

And when you approach the house

Don't walk on by like you always do

Walk in the door

Take a seat

Unfasten your sweater

Uncross your legs

Remove your hat

Unfold your hands

Close your eyes

Hear them

You coward

I FEEL THE HEAVY

I feel the heavy feeling
Of being in the dead man's room
I feel it too
All I have done and not
War-torn
Birth-torn
Into the night
They sought from me
I can't even imagine
What my ancestors endured
All for what
So I go and buy an island
The mosquito buzzes around me
It seeks me
It seeks thee
Me
Ghosts,
I know you seek me
I seek you
You I seek, too
Bees,

I am a walking
Flower goddess
Goodbye,
I said to the air, the sky
Heavy heavy
You are heavy
In my arms,
The sky said to me
I know I am,
Said the bee

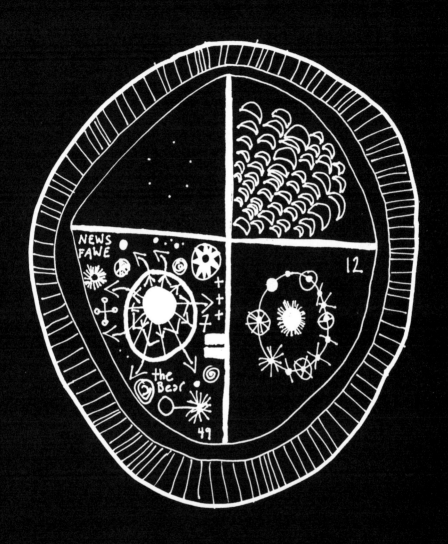

IS IT A BURDEN

Is it a burden to be so perfect
And to have such perfect children
And to have such a perfect marriage
And to look so perfect all the time
And to make every decision perfectly
Cocktails on Thursday with Sammy—perfect
You know your sweater really does look perfect
That mango salad you made—it turned out perfectly
And that car with your shoes
Goddammit that's perfect
Your dog—perfect
Your computer
Well it works perfectly
My supervisor—he's perfect
The desk, it looks perfect
All and all the day was perfect
And lovely and still
What did we do
We walked the earth
So perfect!

Perfect principles
Spring and all
It's perfection
Perfectly ok to be the sallow
Perfect skin and teeth
And shiny hair
And the bathroom clean
The curtains heavy, cream
Hanging to block the noonday sun
Perfectly
The coffin
Light blue
Well that's perfect
The family of worms to eat the face
They did a perfect job
Never coming back here again
I think that seems perfect
Goodbye
Great
Fantastic
Oh all the best
My love to you and yours
Fondly

Finally
Your little heart
Nestled in the air
For all to see
Perfect

THE MEDICAL INSTITUTION

Watching someone die is hard
Watching someone live is even harder
Eight years of sorrow
The rooms full of coats
Everything is about washing your hands
Whatever the reason
My belief in these places is gone
Maybe it's because the nurse said to me
Everything will be fine and then it wasn't
That I lost my ability to care anymore
What people say
If anyone tells you it is fine
Maybe it's Saturday
There is a meal scheduled
But you can get broiled eggplant for ten dollars
Across the street
The attendants who said this will be a simple death
The attendants who said, be strong
Or maybe this scent emanating from the room
Part bleach and part pus

Is the sweetest flower imaginable
Blooming orchid into the seascape
Where we twist through the sands with all the grasses

Instead the stench just keeps growing, wet and unruly
The two friends I actually like visit me
And people stop calling
Until they know for a fact
That she will be better
And maybe sometimes I'm the one who is in the movable cot
Other times I'm in the bed
Some idiot with his need for a fancy dinner
Insists on coming over
With his cigarette-drenched clothes and general filth
Maybe I'm the one on my phone telling others
How she's feeling
Or maybe I'm the one talking
To the drug addicts in the waiting room
Drinking a Coke in the basement by myself
While he sends me a picture of dreams
The town brutal on New Year's Eve
That constant beep of the life machine
Just won't quit

Inside my brain
The doctors call me every day
My goose lays six golden eggs
Into the tumble of the nightwind
With cool desire that glues
For one thousand more we can get you a private room
They tell me
As I bleed into my diaper
And you can have nice food

Maybe because he died in an institution and she didn't
I just keep hoping someone will tell me what death is
What is happening they say
They are screaming
I am too
I tell them
I am screaming too
So loudly
But you can't hear me
Just will someone tell me what life is
Because despite it all
She lived
You know

I am screaming too
Look it's the moon
As bright as the light
Screaming too
But you can't hear me

AGATHA

They are not real
She said from the cellar
And slowly unveiled
The flat scope
Lizards and their eggs
That I hang around the neck
You will break your legs
He warned me
And I believed him
Ruby edgings around
The mushroom-colored stones
And the man who told me
The women
Are like pictures in a book
They are not real
So I believed him
Despite all the years
Finally free
In the end of an era
She held her breasts
On a golden platter

Despite the pain
And blessings everywhere
Eat she said
And they ate
They did

POEM FOR THE MOON MAN

Have some mercy Dottie

No sex, just milk
Is the only thing I have to show for all my hormones

A little vulnerable, not a jerk
Is what he said about you

I am starting to think I am profoundly fucked up

And the only one who can save me is the one I let go in the
river so long ago

Death, death, it's all death

You get to a point where you forget all the people that loved
you
Where all you can do is cry

A time based upon desire

Oh Wolf
Even I forgive you

Oh Moon Man
Even I forgive you

Not a jerk
But a little vulnerable
Young and stupid like everyone else
Slightly concerned with things to the skew of you

Have some Mercy Dottie
Have some mercy world

Be silly Hannah, it's ok
Be silly, girls, it's just us
Take good care, Hilda
It's just us
It's ok to be us
Play and play Hera, go play the day away

No silly, just us

No sex, just milk
Is all we will have to show for it

And if I am insane
And if I am

Then let me be so

Let this skewed version of the world
Always be so

Moon Man
You will always be the nothing of the fall

Let it be so

Let the others run rampant
Let it be so

Dark eyes
And if I'm insane
Let it be so

I am starting to think
Death death

I am starting to really think
Death is all the world has left to offer

And if I am dead
Then let it be so

Forgetting all the people who might have loved me
The blank walls
The marbled walls
The black walls
The night that never ends
The blown-out bits

And if I am so beyond you
Then let it be so
Always darkness and more of it

And if I am darker than light
Then let it be so

I won't look for you Moon Man anymore
I will let you have your life
Go on, go on
Go on, have your life
I won't look for you anymore
I will take my breaths in
I will eat the food they give to me
I will live I will die
I won't search for you anymore
Go there, go on
I am done with you
For good
Moon Man, I am done with you
Go there, go on
The light is waiting
The people, with their arms outstretched
Go to them
I have had enough of you
I won't call on you
Anymore
Moon Man
It's my last plea to you
Leave me

For good
I don't want you anymore

I don't want you
Moon Man
Rounding rounding
A head
Bright and white
Rolling out along the hills
Away from me

BLUE MILK

Green is suffering
Life is suffering
A new life is suffering
You breathe
The air is green
Yellow milk
The moon is pink
The meek is grey
The young are not meek
They live
Life is suffering
Suffering usually
Is unseen
Ghosts are green
They are always alive
Auras are green
The young they suffer
For all eternity
Suffering
Is a green light

ACKNOWLEDGMENTS

Thank you to the editors of the following publications,
who included poems from this book in earlier forms:
Academy of American Poets Poem-a-Day, *Bennington
Review*, *Berkeley Poetry Review*, *Boston Review*, *Granta*,
Lit Hub, *Los Angeles Review of Books*, *Poetry*, *Prac Crit*,
Public Pool, *The Awl*, *The Brooklyn Rail*, *The Creative
Independent*, *The Los Angeles Review*, *The Night Papers*,
The Paris Review, *The White Review*, and *Tin House*.
Thank you to the editors of *Supplement v.2: An Annual
Anthology of Poetry and Innovative Writing* and *A Poetry
Anthology of Women's Resistance* for including some of these
poems in their anthologies. Thank you to Wolfram Swets
and Tungsten Press for originally publishing some of these
poems in a chapbook called *Snakes*. Thank you to Joshua
Beckman for seeing this book into its form and to everyone
at Wave Books for giving this book a home. Special thanks
to my family and friends for all of their love and care.